WHAT'S IT LIKE TO BE A

BABY ELEPHANT?

First published in the UK in 1998 by

 Belitha Press Limited,
London House, Great Eastern Wharf,
Parkgate Road, London SW11 4NQ.

Editor Honor Head
Designer Hayley Cove
Illustrator Matthew Nicholas
Consultants Sally Morgan and Wendy Body

ISBN 1 85561 762 5

British Library Cataloguing in Publication
Data for this book is available from the
British Library

Printed in Belgium

Photo credits Martyn Colbeck/OSF: 16, 18.
Jeanne Drake/Getty Images: 22t.
EIA/Still Pictures: 25. F Hartmann/FLPA: 20, 24.
Chris Harvey/Getty Images: 17.
Martin Harvey/NHPA: 8.
David Hosking/FLPA: front cover & 9.
M & C Huot/Still Pictures: 5r, 11, 13b.
Carla Signorini Jones/Images of Africa: 21, 26.
David Keith Jones/Images of Africa: 14.
Dr M P Kahl/Bruce Coleman Ltd: 19, 29.
Paul Kenward/Getty Images: 27.
Renée Lynn/Getty Images: 30.
Mark Newmann/FLPA: 13t.
Sophy Pilkington/OSF: 22-23.
Leonard Rue/Bruce Coleman Ltd: 10.
Kevin Scafer/NHPA: 28.
Manoj Shah/Getty Images: 5l.
Art Wolfe/Getty Images: 6-7.

The illustrator would like to thank Howletts
Zoo, near Canterbury, for help and advice.

WHAT'S IT LIKE TO BE A

BABY ELEPHANT?

by Honor Head

Illustrated by
Matthew Nicholas

 Belitha Press

In many ways baby elephants are just like human children. They like to play and get up to mischief.

They make lots of noise, they like to chase leaves and birds, and sometimes they are naughty.

Elephants live in Africa and India. The baby elephant in this book is from Africa. Elephants from Africa have bigger ears than those from India. Baby elephants are called calves.

When you read this book imagine that you are a baby elephant. You live in a dry and grassy place where there are lots of other animals. The hot sun shines every day...

You belong to a family group called a herd. Only female elephants live in the herd – mothers, aunts and grandmothers.

Male elephants leave the herd when they are 13 or 14. You probably have three sisters or brothers and lots of cousins.

The other members
of your family were
all there when
you were born.
You could stand
up by yourself
half an hour after
being born.

You are about one
metre tall and weigh
as much as two
grown-up people.

You stay very close
to your mother
until you are about
two years old.

You have a long
nose called a trunk.
You have to be
careful not to
trip over it while
you are learning
how to use it.

You use your trunk for smelling, breathing, eating, saying hello to friends and making loud noises!

You use the tip of your trunk to pick up small things and pieces of dried grass that you might like to munch.

You use your trunk
to hold on to your
mother's tail so that
you don't get lost.

If you fall over,
your mother uses
her long trunk to help
you stand up again.

When you
are naughty,
your mother
nudges you
gently with
her trunk.

If you are in danger the adults in the herd make a circle around you. This is to protect you and the other baby elephants from enemies.

The adults hold out their ears to make themselves look big and scary. They raise their trunks and snort and bellow.

You learn how to
make snorting and
trumpeting noises
with your trunk.

You will do this
to frighten away
enemies when
you are grown up.

15

When you are a bit older
you begin to play with
the other baby elephants.
You enjoy having pretend
fights with them.

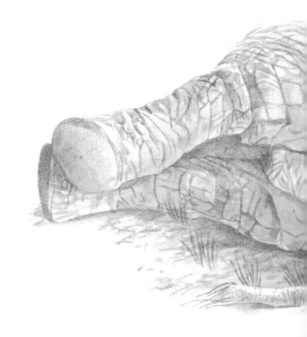

16

You love to chase leaves
and birds. When the
adults are resting,
you like to climb
over them.

Your favourite foods
are grass, fruit,
tree bark, twigs,
roots and flowers.

You eat three times
a day, in the morning,
afternoon and in the
middle of the night.

You drink at least three buckets of water a day.
You have to learn how to suck up water with your trunk and pour it into your mouth.

Until you learn to do this, you put your head in the water and use your mouth to suck up water.

One of your favourite times is bath time. You have fun squirting water at the other baby elephants with your trunk.

After your bath, you cover yourself in mud. The mud helps to protect your skin from tiny insects which bite and make you itch.

You have thick, grey skin and it is very baggy. Your skin is also ticklish! Sometimes your mum tickles you gently with the tip of her trunk.

You have a little
bit of hair on
the top of your
head and on
the tip of
your tail.

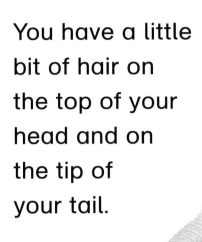

You learn to squirt
yourself with dust.
This helps to keep
your skin soft. It
also helps to keep
you cool.

You have
big ears.
You waggle your
ears backwards
and forwards
to keep cool
in the hot sun.

When it is very
hot, you rest
under a tree
or splash in
cool water.

The sun is bad
for you. It can burn
your skin if you don't
stay in the shade.

The grown-ups
stand over you
to help shelter
you from the sun.

You have only four
teeth at a time.
When one drops out,
another one grows.

Your front teeth
grow into tusks. This
happens when you are
about two years old.

You are too heavy to be able to jump, but you can run quite fast.

After you have run a long way, you like to rest in the shade.

If you are a male elephant you are called a bull. After you leave the herd you live alone most of the time. Sometimes you join other bulls for a short while.

If you are a female elephant, you stay with your family for the rest of your life.

If you are a female elephant you will have your first calf when you are about 12 to 15 years old.

Your first calf will be at least three years old when the next one is born. You may have three or four calves.

When your calves
have grown up
you help the other
mothers to look
after their babies.
You will probably
live for between
50 and 70 years.

INDEX OF USEFUL WORDS

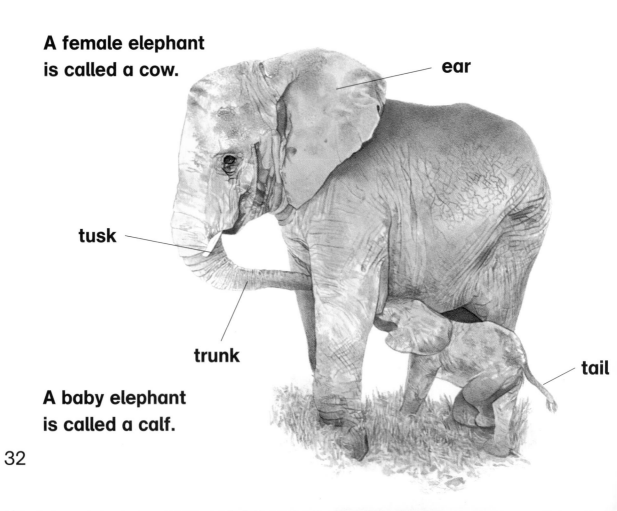

A female elephant is called a cow.

ear

tusk

trunk

tail

A baby elephant is called a calf.

32